Everything You Need To Know
Everything You Need To Know
Everything You Need To Know
Everything You Need To know

George Maliakal

This edition is published in 2016 by

GLAN BOOKS, # 21 Uma Nagar, Thrissur – 680655, Kerala, India.

E-mail : glan221045@gmail.com

ISBN 81 – 87851 – 03 – 1

Acknowledgements:

The Publishers and the Author acknowledge with thanks for the invaluable information that is available in the internet. This vital information is gathered, processed grouped and presented in this book for creating awareness among the public on the subject.

To
My
Family

Table of Contents

1.
INTRODUCTION

Welcome to the World of Online Shopping! Perhaps one might say that it is for the intelligent and the rich people. Well if you think so, then you are mistaken. Though in the beginning, people thought it was something that the common people won't be able to understand. But over the recent years, Online shopping has influenced the life of the people that now people can't live without it. Online shopping has become an integral part of their life. Are you an online shopper already? Then certainly you must have had good and bad experience in online shopping.

What do the families think about shopping? *Most families love to go together for shopping, because, it's the quality time they spend together and it is also great fun.*

But now a days, our life style has totally changed. Every member of the family, both young and old are busy alike. Further, due to worry and tension about the profession, then the time you spent in traffic blocks due to lack of infrastructure, no one has time for anything, especially for family shopping. Therefore, *Online shopping is the ultimate solution to our fast changing 'Life Style'.* And the new *'Visual Commerce Marketpalce'* technology *allows you to walk-through any store and shop while sitting at your home, bringing back the real-life shopping experience',* while maintaining the best customer service.

Online shopping offers fast, easy, money saving and gives you very interesting shopping experience. The best advantage of online shopping is that it gives you 24 hours shopping facility. They also offer you many discounts / offers, you can do your complete shopping from your home, anywhere and anytime and then you will also have a large variety of quality products to choose from.

Furthermore, online shopping is a medium/ lifeline for all those aged, all those who are away from their family living by themselves to get their requirements to their home and for those who are away from their family and friends, to send gifts and other items to their family and friends. Isn't it just amazing?

Online shopping has been really growing very fast all over the world, especially in India. The number of Online Shopping sites in India is really on the increase since then.

Technology has also played a major role in the growth of E-commerce. It would be very interesting to know the growth profile of internet shopping.

The biggest concern is, "How can I find a trustworthy online retail store where I can do my online shopping safe and hassle free. And how and where do I start? Obviously, these questions must be bothering many.

This book, 'Online Shopping - Everything You Need To Know', has everything to make your online shopping a safe, exciting and a thrilling experience.

George Maliakal

2.
ONLINE SHOPPING

2.1   What is Online Shopping?

Online shopping is a form of electronic commerce, also known as e-commerce, which allows consumers to directly buy goods or services from a seller over the Internet using a Web Browser. Other names commonly used for online shopping are: e-web-store, e-shop, e-store, Internet shop, web-shop, web-store, online store, and virtual store etc.

The first online shopping was opened for commercial use in 1991. Later, technological innovations emerged in 1994 for online banking, encryption standard for secure data transfer etc. And the first online shopping system was introduced in 1994. Immediately Amazon.com launched its online shopping site in 1995 followed by eBay, both in US.

Since then, online shopping has been really growing very fast all over the world, especially in India. The number of online Shopping sites operating in India is really on the increase since then. Today we have a large number of online Shopping sites to choose from.

2.2   Online Shopping — Changes Your Life Style

Online Shopping is becoming a necessity in our lives; because it is great help to many like:

    * Aged / sick people living alone can make best use of online shopping. Just order your requirement and the items will be delivered at your doorstep.

    * Disabled people can also make use of the online facility in a similar way.

* Working couples, especially with the new work culture, when they have difficult working hours — living in an almost 'post it pad' situation — difficult to find some common time for their house old needs, online shopping is of great help.
* Those working away from their homes — can send surprise gifts to their near n dear ones using online shopping facility can make their family life more beautiful.
* You can also send flowers / gifts to your beloved ones / friends using online shopping facility.
Isn't it quite amazing?

2.3   Online Shopping makes you Rich!?

Yes. Online Shopping really makes your life Richer in many ways, like:
* **Time Saver** — As compared to the time you spend for your conventional shopping i.e up and down travel time the time you spend for your shopping and also the time you waste in traffic blocks and all, you spend very little time for online shopping.
* **Money Saver** - as compared to the prices of products at the super markets or at shopping malls, you get your products at a much better price with their offers and discounts by shopping online.
* **Additional money saver** — you save money on your travel expenses for the fuel for your car or taxi fare. But if you are doing online shopping. You save money on this.
* **You get a choice** of online shopping sites and also a large number of quality products to choose from.
* **Online shopping is a 24x7** shopping facility unlike the conventional super markets and shopping malls.
* **Very conveniently and comfortably you can do** your online shopping from your home or from a place of your choice.
* **Family shopping** — you can really do a family shopping,

while at your home, where you can seek the views and liking of your family members before selecting the products.

> * **Less traffic jam** – if more and more people change over to online shopping, the traffic on the roads will be considerably and thus reducing traffic blocks.

> * **Air pollution reduced** – lesser the traffic on the roads lesser the air pollution.

> * **Quality Time** – and finally, the time you save by doing online shopping you can add to you 'Quality Time management with your family or for any other useful purposes.

Gain, gain, gain and nothing but gain! Quite unbelievable, isn't it?

So, by shopping online, not only you stand to gain in many ways, but also you help other fellow citizens and your country. Are you guys inspired? Then plan to start your online shopping and we will walk you through the procedures. Pl read the content of this book and everything will be allright.

2.4   Getting Ready for your Online Shopping

Whenever we plan for some event, we always *get ready* to begin that event. On a similar note, here also before you begin online shopping, you must get ready and prepare yourself for that event. And they are:

> * *General awareness* about online shopping,
> * *Open* a *bank account* with internet banking facility,
> * *Avail* a *Credit card or Debit Card* facility from your bank,
> * *Internet connectivity* either at your home, work place or at an Internet Café,
> * *Register yourself* at the site you choose for your online shopping.

But remember, most important point is *'how to identify trust worthy online shopping sites'* for a safe online shopping.

3.
HOW TO MAKE ONLINE SHOPPING SAFE?

Online shopping has been really growing very fast all over the world, especially in India. The number of online shopping sites operating in India is really on the increase since then. Today we have a large number of online shopping sites to choose from.

You need to choose online shopping sites for their trust worthiness with respect to the claims they make about the quality of their products, other offers, their customer care service etc. And this will be a difficult task for many of us.

Doesn't matter. As you continue reading, you will find answers for all your queries and you will be very confident to begin your online purchases. Just remember to read them, understand them and follow these points to ensure your online shopping a safe and thrilling experience.

3 .1   Check their Identity, Location and Contact Details

Check for the identity, location and contact details of the online shopping site. The details should include: the name, company registration details, contact details like their e-mail ID, postal address and telephone number. So that before you make your first purchase from that online shopping site, you can phone or e-mail to the company and clarify any point you would like to and check their response.

Just remember to follow these points to ensure your online shopping a safe and secure experience.

3 .2   Check the Company's Reputation

Check for their *service back-up or returns policies.* You can check this by searching the internet for comments from others on consumer review sites. Read those reviews. Another way to check the reputation of the online shopping site is to check for any complaints through a consumer affair's bureau. Good reviews by the customers and no complaints are good indication of a good online shopping site.

3.3   Check their Billing, Guarantees and Delivery System

Check their Billing, Guarantees and Delivery System before you buy. Always look in for their payment details before sending your credit card details. Look for any *Packaging costs* – shipping charges. Other points you need to check are:

* Whether you will be billed before or after delivery of the products,
* Whether you can track the item from the moment of purchase till the arrival at your door, as this will alert you of any problems in the delivery,
* Whether the product comes with a guarantee or warranty for defects etc,
* How to return the product if it doesn't work or meet your expectations,
* Look for information on the site about their cancellations, returns/ replacements and refund policies.
* Who will bear the cost of returning the item (postage, fees etc.).

3.4   Use a Secured Payment System

Always use a Secured Payment System. If you have chosen the site for your online shopping, ensure that your credit card details are going to be processed using a secure connection.

The most common form of secure encryption is Secure Sockets Layer (SSL). SSL encrypts data and breaks it up into small pieces so that the information cannot be read by anyone wanting to intercept it.

To check that your online shopping site is using SSL or secure technology there are a few things to look for in your Internet Browser:

* Depending on your browser settings you may receive a message stating that you are entering a secure area. The secure area normally begins on the first page where you enter personal details.

* Most often the address bar in your browser will change from starting with http to https. The "s" indicates that the site is secure. But note that often you won't see the "s" until you are on the order page itself.

* You may also find a padlock symbol in your browser, symbolizing the page is secure. The padlock should be closed; if it is open, assume that the site is not secure.

3 .5   Use a Credit Card with Online Fraud Protection

If possible *use a Credit Card with Online Fraud Protection*. Perhaps you know the policy for online fraud protection offered by your credit card company. Many credit card companies offer protection against purchases made without your consent and have special clauses to include online purchases. So make use of such a facility if available.

3 .6   Be Careful While Entering Your Information

You must *be very careful while entering your information*. Be sure to enter the correct details when typing in your order. An incorrect address, amount of items or wrong item code can cause many difficulties. Therefore, always review the information you have entered before you press the send button.

3.7   Read Return/ Replacement of Goods / Refund Policy

Most of the online shopping sites will have their own terms and conditions for returning/ replacement of goods and refund policies. Generally they will differ from site to site. Some of their terms and conditions may look very attractive and reasonable. Here is an example:

"We offer a 30 Day Replacement Guarantee to our customers. If at the time of delivery and /or within 30 days from the date of delivery of the product/s, if any defect is found, then the buyer of the product/s can ask for replacement of the product/s from the seller subject to the following terms and conditions:

1. Notify the seller of any defects in the product/s at the time of delivery of the product/s and/or within 30 days from the date of delivery and the same product/s will be replaced in return of the defective product/s.

2. Replacement can be for the entire product/s or part/s of the product subject to availability of the same with the seller. However the following products shall not be eligible for return or replacement...."

Here again it must be very clearly mention about who will bear the expenses for returning of goods/ reimbursement of such expenses etc. Therefore, it is very important to check in detail the Terms and Conditions of any online shopping sites at least once before selecting a site for your online shopping.

In fact, it is better to avoid than facing such a situation; because it may not be comfortable to anyone. And you can avoid such a situation if you plan your purchase and be sure about the item you want to purchase especially in regard to the size, colour etc.

3 .8   Read the Site's Privacy Policy

Make sure you *read the online shopping site's Privacy Policy.* Reputable companies will be open about how they collect data from you and what they do with it. Look for their privacy policy and learn about whether the company uses your information beyond the purchase transaction, for example, to email you with updates or deals etc. or if it passes on information to third party merchants..

This is how you can end up getting spam mail if you are not careful. So, if the Privacy Policy is not very clear then you must be very cautious in dealing with them. You should avoid such sites and choose other online shopping sites where you are quite satisfied about their Privacy policy.

3 .9   Install a Phishing Filter

If possible try to *install a Phishing Filter.* It will help protect you from phishing sites by warning you when it detects a distrustful website. There are various phishing filters, like Smart Screen Filter in Internet Explorer. E-mail scams that are designed to gather personal information such as passwords and credit card details are known as phishing e-mails.

3 .10   Record Your Purchase Details

Always *record Your Purchase Details.* After purchasing your items, make sure to record the details of the time, date, receipt number and order confirmation. If you cannot print one off, take a screenshot as a form of proof of purchase.

Now here is the summary of all those check points mentioned above.

   * *Check their Identity, Location and Contact Details,*
   * *Find out about the Company's Reputation,*
   * *Check their Billing, Guarantees and Delivery System,*
   * *Use a Secured Payment System,*
   * *Use a Credit Card with Online Fraud Protection,*
   * *Be careful while entering Your Information,*
   * *Read the site's Privacy Policy,*
   * *Install a Phishing Filter and*
   * *Record Your Purchase Details.*

Still if you are not very clear on any of these points then please read though them again.

****

4.
NEW TRENDS IN ONLINE SHOPPING

4.1   Cash on Delivery (COD) – New Payment Option

More and more people across the world are planning to shop online especially in India. At present, most of the online shopping sites in India have credit card, debit card, bank transfers and some other methods that a shopper can use to shop online.

But not everybody has their own credit card to shop online. It is here an easy, convenient and possibly the safest way to shop online come in to play and that is to avail *Cash on Delivery (COD)* as a payment method.

In this Cash on Delivery (COD) system, people can initiate a transaction and buy products without using any credit or debit card. Instead you make the payment when you get the delivery of the items. But this being little risky for the online retailers, most of the online shopping sites that offer COD will verify your credentials before actually starting the process to ship the product.

The process of verification is very simple. What most shopping sites do is that they will send a verification pin to your mobile phone which you'll have to enter on the website. After you successfully enter the pin, your product will be processed for shipping. And when the product reaches your doorstep you'll directly pay to the delivery personnel.

Otherwise, some may ask you to attend a call from them and then they verify you by asking simple questions as your name, address, and the product you bought; and then they will start processing your order. At the time of delivery you or your family can take the delivery and pay cash to the courier personnel.

And this COD system is gaining popularity among the consumers as they need not worry about the security of their online transaction as well as they are sure of receiving quality products as they had ordered.

So your worry about online shopping must be over by now. So begin your online shopping and enjoy the thrilling experience.

COD — The Most Preferred Choice

* Most of the consumers prefer Cash on Delivery (COD) as the payment option for their online shopping. Because,

* Probably, it's the safest payment option.
* You don't want to use your credit/debit card for online transactions.
* Even if you don't have a credit/debit card, you can still do your online shopping and lastly,
* By using COD you can be sure that you get your product before making the payment.

With this, consumers need not worry about the security of their online transaction and more consumers will get attracted to do online shopping.

4 .2   Faster Delivery-Delivery-the heart of online shopping

One of the notable benefits of online shopping is the convenience and time saving as compared to traditional shopping.

It is a fact, online shopping continues to offer opportunities for retailers. But delivery is the key to growing online retail. The boom in online shopping is forcing retailers and logistics firms to adapt to new delivery models to meet customers' needs. It's not simply the price of products, but also the speed and quality of delivery of products to the customers.

And, the time constraint issues, the quality of home delivery services, and the variety of delivery services on offer as some of the reasons why home delivery is the weakest link in the online shopping.

Present Delivery Options

Many traditional and innovative delivery options are currently available to the online retailers, but the situation today is that there is not yet a proven operation model for the home delivery service. The types of delivery methods currently followed are,

* Downloading/Digital distribution: This method is often used for digital media products such as software, music, movies, or images.
* In-store pick-up: The customer selects a local store using a locator software and picks up the delivered product at the selected location
* Drop shipping: The order is passed to the manufacturer or third-party distributor, who then ships the item directly to the consumer, bypassing the retailer's physical location to save time, money, and space.
* Shipping: The product is shipped to a customer-designated address by Self-operated delivery or by a Third-party logistics delivery.

Consumer's Expectations

Most consumers prefer to know about the *expected delivery date of the products*, before purchase. Consumers expect *a flexible delivery window to online shopping*. They want a tracking facility so that they are able to *track the delivery process* and They also want to be informed of the likely time and date of delivery of products.

Future Delivery Trends

Online retailers now know that *delivery of the product* is becoming a significant factor affecting online shopping expansion. The convenience, time saving benefits of online shopping can be offset by increased time in waiting for delivery. Delivery problems could become a bottleneck for the further adoption of online shopping.

Therefore, retailers and logistics firms are having their new trends in order to meet high customer expectations. An appropriate delivery model (or a mix of various delivery methods) needs to be developed to satisfy consumers' different needs.

Factors that affect online retailers to choose which delivery options need to be considered in conjunction with increasing consumer convenience like delivery cost. Delivery models need not only to be convenient to customers but must also financially viable for the company.

4 .3   Better Pricing

With fast changing *Life Style*, consumers have started realizing that *online shopping* is the ultimate solution for their shopping needs. Because, online shopping offers *fast, easy, money saving* and gives you very interesting shopping experience. Therefore, more and more people across the world are getting attracted to online shopping.

Present Pricing Structure

Deals and Special Discounts offers: In order to grab more consumers to their online shopping sites, all possible steps are taken to make the online marketing more attractive. *Deals and*

Special Discounts offers are some of the things the online marketing sites have introduced as part of their sales promotion strategy.

Coupons are another form of discount offered by various online shopping sites to attract more customers to their shopping sites like *Browsing Coupons, Discount Coupons, Drop down Coupons and Gift Coupons* etc.

With these deals/ offers/ coupons you get discounts on your purchases from those shopping sites as per their terms and conditions. So, consumers are very happy about the pricing part of online shopping as they can get products at a much lower price than the market price.

Better Pricing alone attract more consumers?

No, not at all. Though most of the consumers look for a better pricing, they are not prepared to compromise on the quality of products. Also they want a speedy delivery of their products ordered. Consumers are even prepared to pay some extra cost for the delivery options they choose for a safe and speedy delivery of products.

Future Trends in Pricing

Online retailers who understand the concerns and expectations of the consumers should *ensure quality products at a better price with a speedy delivery system* opted by the consumers. Therefore there is a need to revise the present pricing structure.

Since *cash on delivery* (COD) is becoming the most preferred choice by the consumers for a safe online shopping, online retailers should consider the *incidental expenses* connected with COD system while working out their pricing of products.

Products should be priced in such a way, with *special deals and offers*, the price must be very competitive as compared to other online retailers so that more consumers will be attracted to their site.

Such pricing could include free delivery offered by the online retailers. And consumers who choose a particular delivery option could be charged extra.

4.4   Things you should know about Online Pricing

Online pricing of the products are generally on a daily basis or for a limited period offers. Such prices cover their costs and stay in business so you get great deals on exceptional items.

Generally, special discounts are offered:
* As part of their sales promotion strategy, 'less profit and more sales', to create a sudden impact in online shopping.
* Great discounts are also offered during 'festive season' to increase their sales and also during 'off season' to clear their stocks.
* When new products are introduced or launched, to attract more consumers and to increase their sales.
* Compo offers sometimes may look very attractive but such compo offers may include items which you may not interested.
* On a 'stock clearance sale' of items. Such discounted price will apply until all the stock is finished and such items will not be sold again at a higher price.
* On seasonal products so that such seasonal products are sold during that season.
* When there is less or no sales, then prices are reduced on selected items for a while and then jack them back up.
* There is also a possibility for escalating the listed price of certain items and announce special offers to make the pricing more

attractive.

      * Market conditions and competitive pressures may also cause pricing subject to change without further notice.

      * The total payment of an order includes the products' price subtotal, delivery & handling cost and other incidental charges if any.

4.5   Changing Trends - Online Retailing / Shopping

Technology has put consumers everywhere in the power seat, enabling an anytime, anywhere shopping experience. Emerging markets are the growth engines of the retail and consumer goods economy.

Across the world, lower prices, free shipping, and ease of comparison are top reasons for online shopping.

As the customer base is growing fast, some online retailers are increasing their minimum order value to qualify for free delivery.

Many people prefer to do their online shopping through a mobile optimized website over an app; because, it is very convenient, has enough speed and it is easier to use on smart phones.

Consumers have started shopping directly from manufacturers and many no longer distinguish between retailers and their favorite brands.

The direct-to-consumer phenomenon could be one of the biggest stories for both consumer goods companies and retailers in the coming years. Consumers are taking advantage of their newfound ability to connect with manufacturers over the internet.

Looking at the changing trends and fast changing technology, it is difficult for anyone to forecast/ predict the future of online retail and the kind of online shopping in the coming years.

4.6   'Click n Collect' — New Emerging Trend for Online Shopping

With the invent of new technologies and the ever-growing concept of Multi-Channel Retailing having a considerable impact on the customer's daily life, the physical collection of goods by the customer is now a major part of the retail experience.

Consumer expectations about time-saving, personalized service and comfort supported by new technologies are greater than ever.

In this dynamic context, retail chain operators are actively looking for ways to improve their existing service concepts in order to meet their customers' expectations in a better way.

These technologies, which are complementary to ordering at a check out, offer freedom of choice to the consumers. Some people prefer to be served as quickly as possible while others prefer to order serenely without being subjected to the pressure of a queue. By choosing a kiosk service offering, customers can order online and collect their goods from a drive through or collection point at their own convenience.

The intention is to offer various methods of ordering which combine performance and hospitality for the consumer whilst generating an increase in turnover and productivity for the retailer.

Click & Collect — Definition: Click & Collect is the process by which the consumer is able to order online (click) and pick up (collect) their merchandise at a local store or collection point. It is a combination of online and in-store shopping and means the customers can search and buy their products on the internet and pick them up from a location of their choosing.

A Concept to Embrace: The main benefits of Click & Collect for the consumer are savings on delivery costs and choosing a time of collection that suits the customer. Another benefit for the consumer is the convenience of not having to go in-store to find and purchase their goods. Depending on the retailer, the Click & Collect solution may be designed to enable consumers who do not trust online payment solutions to pay at the collecting point.

4.7   Research Online, Purchase Offline – It's A 'ROPO' Trend!

The process of purchasing online is no more a new trend in India. As such, large number of people opts for online shopping.

But deep inside you feel the joy of traditional form of shopping still strikes you at times. Therefore to eliminate the second thoughts with respect to purchasing is revolutionized. The trend changes, from offline to online and goes into transitions when there is a need of hour, a set example is ROPOs.

The trends 'Research Online and Purchase Offline' are now booming in the market with many people deploying this method. There had been few disadvantages while buying the products online, such as shipping of bad quality products delivered at your door step, the online shopping gets restrained if you belong to some rural area and utmost important sometimes products are not that good as they appear to be, i.e. false visualization.

But following the latest trend, ROPO, you get all required information about the products you want to buy including product reviews and price comparison of those products online and finally you can decide on the items and purchase those from selected offline retail store. By doing ROPO, you get quality products at a competitive price, save on shipping charges and above all you get your products when you want. This way you get online experience and enjoy the thrill of traditional shopping. Isn't it amazing?

****

5.
ONLINE SHOPPING — A MOBILE REVOLUTION

Mobile shopping has changed the way we do online shopping, a revolution that is already happening.

Considering that millions of smartphones, tablets already in consumers hands during the last quarter of 2013, the New Year 2014 could be a breakthrough year for mobile shoppers, particularly if businesses continue to adapt to *m-commerce*, engaging their client base with new and innovative methods.

The ongoing mobile revolution is the result of more and more technology in the hands of the consumer, which allow them to virtually window-shop. A large number of Smartphone users look for product reviews, coupons and reductions prior to purchasing anything, frequently while in-store - a consumer trend in shopping, fueled by Social networking.

Mobile is quickly becoming the most preferred e-commerce channel as many online shoppers access multi-channel retailers through a digital channel. Of those mobile shoppers, 30% prefer to use a smartphone or tablet. Also, 50% of online shoppers who own a smartphone and nearly 60% who own a tablet make purchases on these devices. Online shoppers are also open to communications from retailers on their mobile devices. Retailers must prepare themselves for this 'Mobile Revolution'.

Consumer retail growth has done well in 2014 by the rapid growth of *m-commerce* with powerful brands and well-conceived mobile and online commerce strategies.

5 .1   Smartphones the Hero of É-commerce 'Show Business'

The mobile device is increasingly becoming an essential part of the customer's shopping journey. And the ever growing technology is taking 'Mobile Revolution' to another level. The emerging trends highlights, how smartphones usage is becoming more and more popular in many ways, thus making smartphone the 'Hero of the future E-commerce Industry'. And here are some indicating facts.

a) *More Payment options from the retailers:*

We are fast approaching a place where mobile technology will offer retailers something that will create a perfect synergy between payments, loyalty, marketing and advertising.

A new payment solution is under trial that equips retailers with some hardware they can accept EMV cards as well as mobile payments. As retailers increasingly adopt these payment solutions, we can expect more stores to start accepting additional payment types, most notably EMV cards and mobile payments.

b) *Mobile will play a bigger role in click-and-collect initiatives:*

Click & Collect is the process by which the consumer is able to order online (click) and pick up (collect) their merchandise at a local store or collection point. It is a combination of online and in-store shopping and means the customers can search and buy their products on the internet and pick them up from a location of their choosing.

Some online retailers are looking into *using mobile to streamline the in-store pickup experience*. In May 2015, they started testing a service that lets customers text or call their retailer as they near the store. The store employee will then head down and meet the customer outside, so they won't even have to get out of their car. What an innovative thought! These are just a few examples of mobile playing a bigger role in click-and-collect. We can see more such initiatives in 2016. And there are more surprising events in store for everyone. Wait and watch to learn more...

****

6
TABLETS – PREFERRED MOBILE DEVICE FOR ONLINE SHOPPING

Tablets could potentially overtake smartphones as 'preferred mobile device' for online shopping. Tablets are four times more likely to be used for online shopping as compared to smartphones, according to the latest E-commerce Index from online marketplace.

a) *Tablets v/s Smartphones*: According to the global study which looked at the shopping trends of 14 markets, tablet usage grew by 41.9 percent while the use of smartphones saw only a 9.7 percent increase last year.

Just four years after the launch of Apple's iPad, tablets are now fast-becoming the most popular device for shopping online. And with tablet's larger displays offering a more enjoyable experience, makes it more preferred than most smartphones.

b) *PC still reigns*: Despite the growth of mobile commerce, most shoppers still prefer accessing retail sites via PCs. According to the study, 81.8 percent of the shoppers globally shop online using a PC, as opposed to the 13.8 percent who do so through their mobile devices.

In line with the global trend, 82.5 percent of Singaporeans were found to shop online using a PC while only 14.7 percent use a mobile device. Singaporean shoppers were also found to prefer smartphones (8 percent) to tablet (5.4 percent) as their mobile device of choice.

However, with more innovative smartphones with new features and special Apps for online shopping entering the market, it will all depend on the individual's choice as to which one they find it more useful and comfortable to do a 'fast and safe' online shopping.

****

7.
PRODUCT REVIEWS

7.1   Its impact on Online Shopping

One of the great benefits of online shopping is the ability to read others' reviews of a product, by the experts or simply by fellow shoppers. A large number of online shoppers consider reviews prior to their buying. Online reviews and peer recommendations also played a key role for shoppers researching for their future purchases.

A large number of online shoppers say, user-generated customer product reviews have a significant or good impact on their buying behavior.

Further, online reviews are popular for some products and for some particular products like consumer electronics and cars—shoppers mostly trust the recommendations of friends and family most.

Online product research takes up a substantial portion of the time of many consumers spend for their online shopping. According to some study about 50% of consumers spend 75% or more of their total shopping time conducting online product research.

Brand's response to online reviews

A brand's response to an online consumer review changes their perception of a brand, most commonly by making them feel that the brand really cares about customers that it has great customer service and that it is trustworthy. Online shoppers who read brand responses to negative reviews showed significantly higher product sentiment and intent to purchase.

There are different types of negative feedback, of course, which require different responses from brands. Even so, brand responses appear to increase sentiment in each scenario.

7.2   Beware of Fake Online Reviews

Every online retailers are on the lookout for various ways and means to attract more online customers to their sites and thus increasing their sales volume. And online product reviews is one among their action plan. It includes *fake/ sponsored online reviews* on their own sites as well as negative product reviews on other sites.

Considering the importance of online reviews, it is recommended that companies take steps to prevent the growing problem of *fake online reviews*.

It is true online product reviews will certainly help you to select good online retailers as well as to decide on the products that you want to purchase online. But at the same time ii's your own judgment that should matter.

Online reviews and peer recommendations played a key role for shoppers researching for their future purchases. However consumer electronics buyers heavily rely on reviews when making their purchase decisions. They are very much concerned about the authenticity of consumer reviews.

7.3 Evaluation of a Review

Even after an initial judgment of how fair the review is, the following elements also have an impact on their evaluation of a review, like:

* How *well written* is the review,
* Whether the review contains *statistics, specifications,* and other *technical data,*
* Has the *subject matter expertise* demonstrated by the reviewer,
* Number of people who say they found the *review helpful.*

Interestingly, fairness is not top of mind when judging professional reviews. Instead, consumer electronics buyers most likely look at whether the review focuses on aspects/uses of the product that are relevant.

Other Considerations

Consumer electronics buyers are concerned that a positive review may be posted by the manufacturer's employee or agent rather than an actual consumer.

For buyers to doubt a product's quality, they believe that at least a reasonable no. of reviews they see have to be negative.

Many buyers trust the reviews given on Trustworthy Sites and take it for granted while taking their purchase decisions.

The bottom line is, even after all these, if you are confused before making hasty decision, please seek the opinion of other people who can give you correct guidance.

8.
FAKE /GREY MAREKET PRODUCTS

8 .1   Beware of Fake / Grey Market Products

Before you click on the 'buy' button on a great online deal, make sure the products are genuine.

Fakes, grey market imports of reputed brands flourishing in India's and other countries' booming online retail market.

Not every online shopping site is involved in such activities. But then it is becoming a major concern not only for the people of India, but also for the people across the world who love to do online shopping.

Many Brand leaders have already initiated legal actions and have started warning customers to negotiating with top retail portals to deal with the menace.

Online listing of fake and refurbished products impacts their brand equity as well as the overall credibility of online retail industry.

Fake/ refurbished products are being pushed through as Branded products and are being sold at much lower price under the cover of 'special deals / offers' etc. And people get attracted at such offers believing it to be a great deal for buying a branded product at such a low price without knowing that they are being cheated by someone in some way.

While fashion brands are worried about fakes, consumer electronics and gadgets makers are concerned about parallel imports and refurbished products being sold as new.

Most online retailers say online pricing is a headache for them. And rising competition among the online retailers to increase their customer base as well as their sales volume, make some of the online retailers to choose product suppliers who supply them products at a cheaper rates than from the their authorized dealers without realizing such products are fake or genuine. And online shoppers looking for branded products at a much lower price often fall into such traps.

This kind of malpractices if not checked in the beginning, this can go viral and the damage could be beyond anyone imagination, as it will have its adverse effects both on online retailers as well as the online shoppers.

8 .2   Fake Products Flood the Online Retail Market

Before you click on the 'buy' button on a great online deal, make sure the products are genuine. Because, fakes, grey market imports of reputed brands are flooding everywhere and in India's booming online retail market.

According to a recent study by industry body Assocham, the fake luxury market in India is growing at a 40-45 per cent rate annually and is likely to more than double to Rs. 5,600 crore from the current level of about Rs. 2,500 crore. The body has further said that several web shopping portals account for over 25 per cent of the fake luxury goods market in India.

Not every online shopping site is involved in such activities. But then it is becoming a major concern not only for the people of India, but also for the people across the world, who love to do online shopping.

Many Brand leaders have already initiated legal actions and have started warning customers to negotiating with top retail portals to deal with the menace.

Online listing of fake and refurbished products impacts their brand equity as well as the overall credibility of online retail industry.

a) *How this is done?*
Fake/ refurbished products are being pushed through as Branded Products and are being sold at much lower price under the cover of 'special deals / offers' etc. And people get attracted at such offers believing it to be a great deal for buying a branded product at such a low price without knowing that they are being cheated by someone in some way.

A big chunk of the market for fake luxury goods is constituted by accessories such as watches, handbags, sunglasses, perfumes and jewelry. And this market is growing at a rate twice that of the market for genuine luxury goods.

While fashion brands are worried about fakes, consumer electronics and gadgets makers are also concerned about parallel imports and refurbished products being sold as new.

b) *Unhealthy competition:*
Most online retailers say online pricing is a headache for them. Rising competition among the online retailers to increase their customer base as well as their sales volume, make some of the online retailers to choose product suppliers who supply them products at a cheaper rates than from the their authorized dealers without realizing such products are fake or genuine. And online shoppers looking for branded products at a much lower price often fall into such traps.

c) *Future impact*:

According to recent reports 'fake luxury products' market in India is Rs 2,500-3,000 cr. and is expected to grow more than double to Rs. 5,600 crore. Isn't it quite alarming?

This kind of malpractices if not checked in the beginning, this can go viral and the damage could be beyond anyone imagination, as it will have its adverse effects both on online retailers as well as the online shoppers.

So before you click on the 'buy' button on a great online deal, make sure the products are genuine; because it is your hard earned money.

8.3   How to prevent Fake Products?

Fake/ refurbished products are being pushed through as Branded products and are being sold at much lower price under the cover of 'special deals/ discounts/ offers' etc. And people get attracted at such offers believing them to be a great deal for buying a branded product at such a low price without knowing that they are being cheated by someone in some way.

Experts say it's not easy to make a fool-proof system because several online websites have their back-end servers located outside the country. Not every online shopping site is involved in such activities. However if this kind of malpractices of fake/ grey market products is not checked in the beginning, this practice can go viral and the damage could be beyond anyone imagination as it will have its adverse effects both on online retailers as well as the online shoppers.

8.4   Possible Practical Solution

The only possible practical solution to this problem is to :

* Create product awareness among the people.
* Gain the trust n confidence of the people.
* Online retailers should ensure that they buy quality and original products from the authorized dealers of the manufactures.
* Beware of 'independent / multi-product marketing agencies who offer products at much lower rates than the minimum selling price.
* The Governments should take appropriate steps and pass stringent laws to check fake/ grey market products from entering their markets.

Now a days, consumers are taking advantage of their newfound ability to connect with manufacturers over the Internet. They can also shop directly from the manufacturers and many no longer distinguish between retailers and their favorite brands.

The direct-to-consumer phenomenon could be one of the biggest events for both consumer goods companies and retailers in the years.

9.
PRICE COMPARISION SITES (PCS)

9.1   PCS offer you the Best Price?

The new concept of online shopping is the use of Price Comparison sites. Price comparison sites cover a wide of consumer items, but well-known sites tend to specialize in financial products such as insurance, credit cards, personal loans and gas and electricity tariffs.

Billions of people across the globe use price comparison websites before they actually decide to buy a product; because they're quick, convenient and save us a lot of time shopping around. But not many of us really know that we're paying a huge sum a year in commission for this privilege.

Price comparison sites give the impression that they scour the whole market to find you the cheapest 'best buy' products. But that often isn't the case. Most of us rely on comparison sites to find a better deal, but they can be confusing.

9.2   PCS Save you Quality Time?

Time is Money - Time is the essence of everything — and Quality Time — is the most precious time of your personal life — the time you love to spend for your own personal needs, with your family and friends and even with your pet, if you have any.

With this new concept of 'Price Comparison sites, while doing online shopping there's no need to phone a friend frantically to make sure you're getting the lowest price possible; your phone can tell you.

While most of shoppers are looking for comparison of prices, some of the sites also provide 'product reviews'. And some Price Comparison sites have gone even a step further, by providing 'Buyer's Guide' for the product you choose to buy. All these features give you answers to your questions you would like to know before you buy the product online, thus making your online shopping more exciting and thrilling experience.

9.3   How do PCS work?

Price comparison sites are designed to do just what their name implies: compare the price of goods and services from a range of providers. Price comparison sites are commonly used to compare financial products. This allows the consumer to make an informed decision about which provider to choose in order to save money.

Price comparison sites cover a wide of consumer items, but well-known sites tend to specialize in financial products such as insurance, credit cards, personal loans and gas and electricity tariffs.

Price comparison websites specialized in products such as car, home and travel insurance, allow the consumers to get quotes from a variety of insurance firms in a single stroke, thus avoiding the need to fill in multiple sets of forms and make enquiries about what's on offer from the market's vast array of insurers.

Some of these sites also let you search hundreds of deals from providers large and small in the credit card, mortgage and savings markets to choose a great deal based on quality of service as well as cost and benefits.

9.4   How to use Price Comparison Sites?

Never rely on a single price comparison site. You must be aware that no two price comparison websites are likely to yield exactly the same results – even if you provide them with identical information. This is because they may provide quotations from different financial product providers and insurers, depending on which companies they have access to.

Price comparison websites tend not to have a 'whole of market' focus, which means most sites will miss out some possible deals when providing you with quotations.

For this reason, 'money experts' would always advise against using a single price comparison site when trying to track down the best price you can find for a product such as insurance.

Likewise there are certain issues you might encounter when using price comparison sites. These can affect the level of cover you receive when buying insurance, the excess you are expected to pay and could see your email inbox clogged up with marketing messages.

The bottom line is that you should never rely on the results of a single price comparison site, but try and check a couple of other price comparison sites and look for the best option. Anyways, you are the judge and the final decision is yours to accept the suggestion or not.

9.5   Tips for using Price Comparison Websites —

Using price comparison websites is a smart way to compare the financial products you have with the newer, better deals that might be out there. What's more, they can make the process simple and easy.

Always use Price Comparison websites very carefully to ensure you get the right deals. Now, here are some important Tips that you should follow while using a Price Comparison website.

a) *Don't use just one price comparison site*

As most people are aware, price comparison sites can't claim to cover the whole market for the very best financial products in every category. For this reason, it makes sense to use several price comparison sites before choosing which product to take out.

It's also worth remembering that some financial product providers choose not to be featured on price comparison sites.

To compare products from companies that don't subscribe to comparison sites, you'll have to get quotes from them individually - although this shouldn't take more than a few minutes per firm and could be well worth the effort.

Although it takes a little more time to use several comparison sites and look at what the companies have to offer, this is the best way to make sure you don't lose out on the best deal.

b) *Beware assumptions that could invalidate your insurance*

Some price comparison websites will make assumptions about your circumstances when you visit them for a quote. In many cases these may be appropriate to your needs - but be careful to keep an eye on them, as some people will find the 'standard' situations used by comparison sites when serving up quotations do not apply to them.

If you've used a price comparison website and aren't completely confident that the deals it has presented you, are right for your circumstances, phone the product provider directly to be sure.

c)   *Make sure the right boxes are ticked*

Pre-ticked boxes often feature on price comparison websites – and ignoring them, or failing to amend what has been pre-selected for you, could have serious consequences.

It isn't unusual, for example, for a price comparison website to assume that you do not have a criminal record and pre-tick a box stating that you have no convictions – but if you have been convicted of an offence in the past and don't untick the box yourself, you could be left with an insurance policy that won't pay out when you need it to.

Likewise, some price comparison websites pre-tick boxes agreeing that customers will pay for financial products such as car insurance either annually (in one lump sum) or monthly (usually by direct debit).

Paying for insurance monthly is often the most expensive option, so you may want to avoid this if you can – but equally, not everyone will be able to afford to pay their entire insurance premium up-front, so be sure to check whether the site you are using has pre-selected either option, and to choose the one that suits you.

d)   *Consider quality as well as cost.*

Finally, it's worth remembering that price comparison websites are set up to find customers the cheapest possible deals when it comes to products like car and home insurance – and this may mean you don't get the level of cover you would expect, or benefit from the standard of customer service you would like.

Quality is as important a cost, so it makes sense to focus on getting value for your money - not the very cheapest deals - when you buy financial products. Remember that low-cost insurance policies, for instance, are unlikely to include perks such as the provision of a replacement hire car should your vehicle be damaged in an accident. In a tight spot, you might appreciate benefits like this even if they cost a little more.

Many experts have assessed car and home insurance policies based on the quality of the cover on offer as well as how much they will set you back, and have come up with a list of recommended providers of each.

9.6   How do the Price Comparison sites make money?

Comparison websites make their money in a number of ways.

        * The simplest and most obvious is from advertising on the website.
        * A second income stream comes from sponsored listings, whereby companies pay to have their products appear at the top of search results.
        * The third revenue stream comes from click- through where the comparison site earns referral commission when a customer clicks through to a company's website and buys a product.
        * The sites also make a lot of money in commission from the companies that list products on their websites.
A recent survey found that consumers thought they paid between 5% and 10% in commission when they bought something through a comparison website; but in reality, the average commission is around 24%. If a Price comparison site can convert more people from lookers into buyers, the more income it will earn.

9.7   Confusing Facts you MUST know

Consumers using Price Comparison sites assume they will be presented with the cheapest deals. In reality, however, the firms put up hurdles which make it more difficult to find cheap deals from small power firms that do not pay commission.

Price comparison websites have been accused of keeping customers in the dark about the cheapest energy deals. Householders are pushed away from rivals who are offering better value options

They are said to be pushing householders towards big energy firms that pay the sites millions of pounds in commission and screening out cheaper rivals that do not.

Many families are unaware the switching websites get a commission — generally £50-£70 — for each customer who moves their account.

Price Comparison sites can screen out cheaper deals by asking if you are interested in switching to a new energy supplier 'today'. If you click 'Yes', it will flag up all those deals and tariffs which the site can connect you to. The website will generally be paid a commission — typically £50-£70 — by the energy firm you switch to.

If you click 'No' you will also be given a longer list of companies that could be cheaper, but with no direct link to their websites. Often these cheaper tariffs come from companies that do not pay commission to comparison sites.

The comparison sites do provide a link to explain how they make their money, but they talk about a 'small commission' rather than stating the exact figure.

By using 'Price Comparison sites' in a way, you save a lot of your time in identifying and finally selecting the product you are looking for at the lowest price offered anywhere online, best deal / offers, Payment system, best delivery, may be with free shipping and with product return guarantee - in short, a purchase with maximum purchase benefits.

9.8   Top Ten Shopping Apps to Compare Prices

If you are not sure of getting the best price available for the product, these barcode-scanning Apps can help you to find the best price for the product you would like to buy. These Apps will also let you know if the item is a deal or no deal before you make a costly mistake.

So, while shopping there's no need to phone a friend frantically to make sure you're getting the lowest price possible; your phone can tell you. While most of shoppers are looking to compare prices, some of them also like to check product reviews.

With price-comparison apps on your smartphone, you need to merely to snap a barcode and perform a search. Here are some of the Top Shopping Apps you can chose from to make your online shopping more exciting and thrilling experience.

a) RedLaser: Scan a barcode with RedLaser and you're locked into information from retail and online stores. It keeps more cash in your wallet while also lightening it by storing loyalty cards. This Apps are available on iOS, Android, Windows Phones.

b) ShopSavvy: Tell the app what you're looking for and it'll keep an eye out for when you can get it at a discount. You can also see when there are sales at major stores. ShopSavvy also works as a barcode scanner and SKU finder. It is available on iOS, Android,

Windows Phones.

c) BuyVia: Buying a tech gift? Download BuyVia to your iOS or Android device. It compares prices at national and local outlets and lets you set up alerts (including location-based) for products. At a store to be sure if the price on the shelf is the lowest, use the UPC barcode scanner to get an answer on the spot. It is available on iOS, Android phones.

d) Smoopa: Smoopa gives you the go-ahead to buy in stores after letting you scan an item's barcode and compare it against online prices. If the store has the best deal, it displays a green button. If it doesn't, you're cautioned against buying with a yellow button and shown online options, available on iOS, Android phones.

e) The Find: Bar-code scan is your way to a deal with The Find. This app only locates nearby deals and what's available online, limiting results to only what's useful. You can set price alerts for when items you're interested in hit the sweet spot, available on iOS, Android phones.

f) PriceGrabber: Searching online deals isn't a manual process with PriceGrabber. The app lets you search online stores for deals and compare in-store prices to online ones using a barcode scanner. It is available on iOS, Android phones.

g) Consumr: Scan the items to compare prices and get info. Consumr is a great source of user reviews too. If you choose to review products, you can also earn rewards. It's available on iOS phones.

h) ScanLife: You can compare prices online and locally with ScanLife. ScanLife also has real-life user reviews of products, can share your finds on Facebook, and lets you earn rewards in the form of gift cards. It is available on iOS, Android phones.

j) ShopAdvisor: When to buy can be as important as what to buy. ShopAdvisor watches price changes so you don't have to. Apart from price comparisons, you can set up an alert for when an item reaches the price you're willing to pay for it. Besides from scanning items in stores, you can also scan from magazines. It's available on iOS, Android phones.

k) Walmart Savings Catcher: Walmart Savings Catcher is a feature of Walmart's regular app. After shopping at Walmart, you can use it to scan your receipt and compare prices of some items against competitors' advertised deals and get the difference back on a Walmart Rewards eGift Card. It's available on iOS, Android phones.

Excited? So, choose a 'price comparison apps' that you like and make your future online shopping more exciting and thrilling experience.

9.9   Most Popular Price Comparison Shopping Sites:-

Price comparison sites are designed to do just what their name implies: compare the price of goods and services from a range of providers. Price comparison sites are commonly used to compare financial products. This allows the consumer to make an informed decision about which provider to choose in order to save money.

Price comparison sites cover a wide of consumer items, but well-known sites tend to specialize in financial products such as insurance, credit cards, personal loans and gas and electricity tariffs.

To make things easier for you, here are some of the top most popular Price comparison shopping sites. But remember to follow the Tips for using Price Comparison sites. They are listed as per their popularity as of now, which may change according to their performance.

http://www.google.com/shopping Most popular Price Comparison Shopping sites: Alexa Global rank as on April 09, 2015 – 1 (ONE) and Rank in United States – 1 (ONE)

http://slickdeals.net/ Most popular Price Comparison Shopping sites: Alexa Global rank as on A

April 09, 2015 – 291 and Rank in United States – 78

http://www.woot.com/ Most popular Price Comparison Shopping sites: Alexa Global rank as on April 09, 2015 – 473 and Rank in United States –158

http://www.coupons.com/ Most popular Price Comparison Shopping sites: Alexa Global rank as on April 09, 2015 – 873 and Rank in United States – 266

http://www.fatwallet.com/ Most popular Price Comparison Shopping sites: Alexa Global rank as on April 09, 2015 – 1511 and Rank in United States – 521

http://www.shop.com/ Most popular Price Comparison Shopping sites: Alexa Global rank as on April 09, 2015 – 1947 and Rank in United States –40

http://dealnews.com/ Most popular Price Comparison Shopping sites: Alexa Global rank as on April 09, 2015 – 1979 and Rank in United States –573

http://www.shopathome.com/ Most popular Price Comparison

Shopping sites: Alexa Global rank as on April 09, 2015 - 2570 and Rank in United States — 847

http://www.bizrate.com/ Most popular Price Comparison Shopping sites: Alexa Global rank as on April 09, 2015 - 3539 and Rank in United Sta http://www.nextag.com/ Most popular Price Comparison Shopping sites: Alexa Global rank as on April 09, 2015 - 6627 and Rank in United States — 4475

http://www.shoplocal.com/ Most popular Price Comparison Shopping sites: Alexa Global rank as on April 09, 2015 - 5074 and Rank in United States — 1124

http://www.shopping.com/ Most popular Price Comparison Shopping sites: Alexa Global rank as on April 09, 2015 - 7946 and Rank in United States — 1574

http://www.pronto.com/ Most popular Price Comparison Shopping sites: Alexa Global rank as on April 09, 2015 - 9025 and Rank in United States — 2895

 http://www.pricegrabber.com/ Most popular Price Comparison Shopping sites: Alexa Global rank as on April 09, 2015 - 10329 and Rank in United States — 4471

http://www.shopzilla.com/ Most popular Price Comparison Shopping sites: Alexa Global rank as on April 09, 2015 - 13981 and Rank in United States — 6390

9.9   Popular Price Comparison Sites for Shopping in India

Checking Price Comparison sites to find out the best price for a product has become the call of the day. Price comparison sites cover a wide range of consumer items, but well-known sites tend to specialize in financial products such as insurance, credit cards, personal loans and gas and electricity tariffs.

To make things easier for you, here are some of the most popular Price Comparison Shopping Sites in India; but before you start using them, please read through my earlier post on ' Tips for using Price Comparison Websites'. They are listed as per their popularity as of now, which may change according to their performance.

Where-to-buy.in: Where-to-buy is providing a dynamic interface to search or browse products, features and prices.

Sulekha.com: Sulekha is a portal offering so many services and mobile price comparison is a section of this portal.

Junglee.com: Junglee is from Amazon, it is India's largest price comparison site. It has a large range of products in catalogue and you get multiple choices in price competition.

Mysmartprice.com: Mysmartprice recently become a popular price comparison site in India, homepage is full of mobile phones but you can compare other products as books, cameras, electronics and home appliances.

91mobiles.com: 91mobiles was a mobile reviews site but now it has added price comparison feature.

Pricedekho.com: Pricedekho is a popular website for comparison. You can compare prices for mobiles, cameras, mp3 players, TV and laptops.

Pricecheckindia.com: Pricecheckindia is another price comparison site for cameras, mobiles phones, televisions etc.

Pricedealsindia.com: Pricedealsindia is also a popular website, on homepage you can see four products in a row, and you can see the price for TV, camera, mobile phone, MP3 player, external hard disk and tablets.

Mypriceindia.com: Mypriceindia is for mobile, laptop and camera price comparison.

Pricesbolo.com: Pricesbolo is a small website in popularity but it has a large range of products for comparison.

On a similar lines, there are well-known sites specialized in financial products such as insurance, credit cards, personal loans and gas and electricity tariffs. And you must also check the most popular 'Price Comparison sites for Financial Products' in India before taking any action.

9.10 Most Popular PC sites for Financial Products in India

Checking Price Comparison sites to find out the best price for a product has become the call of the day. Price Comparison sites cover a wide of consumer items and some sites specialize in financial products such as insurance, credit cards, personal loans and gas and electricity tariffs.

You can compare and apply for Loans, Credit Cards and Insurance and get good deal without agent calling or speaking to anyone!

Here are some of the most popular Price Comparison Sites for Financial Products in India; but before you start using them, please read through my earlier post on 'Tips for using Price Comparison Websites'. They are listed as per their popularity as of now, which may change according to their performance.

Bankbazaar.com: BankBazaar simplifies your personal finance &

help you get your Best Loans in India. Need to research or apply for Loans, Credit Cards or Insurance Products? Apply online for Special Offers, Lowest Interest Rates Do research, Get a quote, Check your eligibility and compare Best Life Insurance Plans in India.

Policybazaar.com: Policybazaar.com compare online, insurance policies offered by various insurers of India and helps you compare Insurance Quotes Online: Life | Car | Health | Travel. So, compare and apply for Loans, Credit Cards and Insurance and get good deal without agent calling or speaking to anyone!

Ratekhoj.com: Ratekhoj is a newly launched comparison service for financial products and enables one. Looks good and one can select multiple products in a category and compare them.

Paisabazaar.com: Paisabazaar Apply Online for Best Loans in India at lowest interest rates, best loan offers and low EMI. Check eligibility, Use Loan & EMI Calculators & get quotes instantly.

Apnapaisa.com: ApnaPaisa offers price comparison services for products such as Home loan, car loan, personal loan, loan against property, loan for education and also gets you various insurance proposals like life, health and car insurance.

Myinsuranceclub.com: Compare and get free premium quotes for the best life insurance, health insurance, travel insurance and car insurance plans in India at MyInsuranceClub.com. It is a Great way to save money over the longer term. There are more than 20 life insurance companies with very different kinds of plans and their corresponding features.

So it is always worthwhile to understand everything about 'Price Comparison sites' so that you can use their services for your online shopping, with which you will be able to save money and a lot of your time. And the time thus saved is your additional quality time, which you can spend for yourself, with your family and friends and pets and thus making your life more beautiful and colorful.

10.
LATEST GLOBAL TRENDS

10 .1   Using Data to Revolutionize Shopping Experience

Customers now expect to be able to shop 24x7, discover and buy products on multiple online and offline channels, look for ideas and inspiration on brands' social media channels, increasingly shop on mobile devices and demand more customized experiences when they walk into a store.

Therefore, now, more than ever before, retail brands need to become more customer-centric and analytically-driven. Retail brands realize that to win and retain loyal customers, they need to focus more on the customer relationship than the products and access to big data. And the new marketing technologies are helping them make this transition easier.

a) **Fashion wear**: Many top stores provide '*virtual fitting rooms*', so that the customers can select specific garments and see how they would look wearing those garments on large screen. This makes the whole process of selection, trials and decision making very simple and faster.

b) **Cosmetic Mirrors**: Japanese beauty retailer Shiseido is using new technology to create digital shopping experiences in their Tokyo stores. Their much-hyped '*cosmetic mirrors*' are digital screens that a customer can use to scan product barcodes and see a virtual image of her faces with that product virtually applied to it.

This amazing new way of digital trying on makeup without having to actually apply it on their faces allows customers to sample multiple products without the hassle of remove the sampled makeup multiple times.

These *"cosmetic mirrors"* also provide beauty advice, product recommendations and printouts of before-and-after photos and shopping lists. White these digital mirrors are already being used at multiple stores in Japan, these are yet to be introduced in their U.S. stores.

c) *Image Recognition Technology*: The world's leading furniture retailer, IKEA, prints more than 210 million catalogues in 60+ languages each year, driving thousands of people to their websites and physical stores. In 2013, the IKEA catalog featured ' *Image recognition and Augmented Reality'* for the first time ever offering personalized digital content and product views to customers, and for merging the benefits of in-store and online shopping.

With IKEA's *'Image-Recognition Technology'*, readers can scan the catalog with their mobile devices to see relevant content including a '360-view' furniture displays.

More importantly, customers can "virtually" place IKEA furniture pieces in their own homes to choose the products, color and sizes that work best, without having to actually go into a store. Isn't it quite amazing?

With more and more new technologies coming in, we are moving into a wonder-world where shopping, whether online or offline compete against each other to attract and retain more and more consumers.

10 .2   Shopping through Social Networks

Facebook now ranks first for traffic generation among all the websites on the Internet? Do you believe it? Well people say, it even beats out Google?

The number of Facebook users is increasing with each passing day. Right now, it is told, there are approximately 500 million active users on Facebook. Imagine the increase in the volume? Perhaps it is much more than the population of many countries in the world. It is the concept of Facebook marketing that has given rise to this immense popularity.

Online retailers are very quick to latch on to the immense popularity of Facebook. They know that if they make a presence here, they can showcase their business to the outside world. They are trying to build a creditable network, a fan base for their business that they can tap into for their business profits.

One of the things that they do is to create a professional business page for themselves instead of the routine profiles that people create on Facebook. And with the recent applications like FBMaxed, it is possible for Internet entrepreneurs to place their entire website onto their Facebook profile. This helps them create the right impression in their market and they can even make these websites with clickable URLs so that interested people can go and visit their site. These websites can embed videos right into the Facebook profile page itself. All these developments do make a huge difference.

With the great popularity of Facebook, the concept of Facebook marketing has gained in strength as well. People are now coming to Facebook with the idea of finding a good product that they would like to invest in. It also gives them a chance to discover a new product and check out the reviews from their Facebook friends.

Online shopping has been really growing very fast all over the world, especially in India. The number of Online Shopping sites in India is really on the increase since then.

Technology has also played a major role in the growth of E-commerce. It would be very interesting to know the growth profile of internet shopping.

10 .3   What is 'Visual Commerce'?

Technological contribution to the field of E-commerce has been tremendous. And technology has been stretching further beyond our imagination. The latest technology being '*Visual Commerce*' and '*Visual Commerce Market Place*'.

E-commerce will become more visual. In the future, the customer journey can begin with an image-based search. More recently, *visual commerce* has been used to discuss innovative approaches to visual merchandising by companies such as Amazon.com and L'Oreal.

It's a unique technological solution that introduces the concept of Visual Commerce to bridge the gap between the online and offline retail, providing the real feel of offline shopping to the families while they shop online from their home. This technology allows the shoppers to walk-through any store and shop while sitting at your home.

The *Visual Commerce Engine, is a virtual tour, virtual reality, virtual shop and virtual store technology based system. This can be integrated with any E-commerce system to enable visual commerce and virtual 360 shopping. It's an augmented reality commerce solution for offline retailers.*

This technology provides great opportunity to large offline retailers to add more sales through both offline and online as well.

Any retail store can now reach millions of customers across the globe. Similarly customers get the option of browsing through stores, enquiring about products directly with the store, rate individual stores, share comments and engage with their favorite retailers.

Visual Commerce is a revolution in the way that *E-Commerce websites display and sell products online*. With the advent of new and innovative technologies, the future of e-commerce is quite unpredictable. We can expect more and more exciting features in the future.

10 .4   What is "Conversational Commerce"?

Conversational commerce is transforming the "messaging app", as we know it, into so much more. Conversational commerce minimizes the user interface and ultimately creates the simplest experience possible. Instead of having to use many apps, each with their own branding and logos and designs and interfaces, you'll be able to leverage these services all via a single chat interface. This takes the pain out of having to use, and get used to, multiple apps.

Imagine a world where you could open a messaging app—on your choice of device—and type or speak: What you want. Say, I need a dress for my daughter to wear on a special occasion, under $150. And in seconds, you get a message back—"Here is the dress"—with a link to a personalized product recommendation along with express shipping selected, your choice of color, and your size already accounted for, which you can then pay for, and track the shipping status, without ever leaving the conversation.

This is just one example of conversational commerce in action and how it will changing the way we buy things— the way your business will interact with its customers.

a) *Conversational Commerce how useful?* The introduction of apps using these text interfaces marks a visible shift in user behavior.

Messaging Apps as a Channel to Communicate with Customers: Chat is already a popular channel for customers to engage with a business in private.

Messaging Apps as a Way to Pay: Payments are at the heart of all forms of commerce, whether business-to-consumer, business-to-business or peer-to-peer. As such, it's also one of the areas of focus in this shift towards conversational commerce.

Messaging Apps as Your Personal Assistant: On the consumer side, it's the new services enabled by conversational commerce that will really change the way we buy.

Messaging Apps as your App for Everything: We can speculate all we want about the future of conversational commerce. WeChat—a popular messaging app in China—has already entrenched itself as the go-to app for everything.

b) *The Era of Conversational Commerce is already here...*

The convenience this affords consumers, from removing the burden of pre-purchase research to making payments only a few taps away, will build upon the already existing foundations laid by mobile and social commerce—in a big way.

In a word, conversational commerce is bringing commerce into the familiar and personal context of messaging apps, transforming the customer experience by making it a whole lot more convenient for both businesses and their customers alike.

If you're looking for it on the distant horizon, you're looking the wrong way. Because the era of conversational commerce is already here.

c) Conversational Commerce — the new trend for consumer computing apps

'Conversational Commerce' is one of 2016's most promising technology trends, utilizing chat, messaging, or other natural language interfaces (i.e. voice) to interact with people, brands, or services and bots. Conversational commerce is an exciting shift in the world of tech and business.

11.
E-COMMERCE AND LOGISTICS

11.1   Growing E-Commerce a bon for Logistics Sector

The race to *sort, package and ship* millions of products that Indians are buying online is becoming a hotly contested one in the Indian logistics industry as several companies launch innovative services to grab the growing business. The lack of efficient logistics support has been a bottleneck for India's online retail industry.

DotZot in which DTDC one of the largest logistics companies in India holds a majority stake will set up collection centers in urban and rural locations where consumers can pick up packages and drop off the ones they want to return. The company, which is now on track to earn Rs 20 crore this fiscal and Rs. 100 crore by 2016, uses DTDC's extensive network covering over 5,200 locations in India to deliver 12,000 shipments a day.

Also in the fray for a slice of this growing action are specialist startups like Delhivery and Ecom Express that are preparing to launch more focused services for the e-commerce industry. These ventures will set up warehouses with machines sorting out thousands of parcels and at the other end provide alterations at a customer's doorstep.

11.2   Innovations vital to meet customer expectations:

Such innovations have become vital to meet customer expectations in an industry that doubled in size within a year to reach Rs 12,500 crore last year. By 2023, online retail is expected to become a $56 billion (almost Rs 3.5 lakh crore) industry. Every single online retail transaction needs to be delivered.

Other large firms like Blue Dart and Aramex have also set up separate ecommerce divisions to take on the challenges. A study showed that online retail will add $5 billion (over Rs 31,000 crore) annually to the income of logistics companies by 2021. In the next year just Snapdeal will generate business of about Rs 250 crore for 'third party logistics' (3PL) firms according to its cofounder Rohit Bansal.

a) Collection — Delivery — Return of Goods:
Logistics companies have so far had to catch up to meet the basic requirements in this fast-growing industry. They have now established systems and processes to pick up packages from a number of sellers and ship them to multiple pin codes.

b) Tracking Systems:
At a customer's doorstep they pick up returns and keep the online retail firms updated on the status of the package at every step of its journey. Even cash-on-delivery (COD), which accounts for about 60% of all online retail transactions, is under control, said the companies.

IT systems are built to track COD and have worked with partner banks to remit the money to their branches, sometimes multiple times a day. Delhivery, which aims to earn Rs 60 crore this fiscal, was founded in 2011 and has a reach of 130 cities. Delhivery, which has an employee base of 3,000, handles about 50,000 orders a day.

c) Driving Innovation:
With competition heating up in online retail, companies have started

offering services like next-day and same-day deliveries, adding to the pressures on logistics companies. The need for speed and the requirement to reach customers in remote locations is driving innovation. If online retail has to grow to the humongous numbers everyone is talking about then logistics has to reach the smaller towns.

DotZot is running a pilot for drop off points in Delhi and a few smaller cities like Rajkot. Here a customer can return a package at designated collection centres, where they are scanned by staff resulting in instant returns message to the customer and the online site.
The company is intending to launch a similar facility for pickups. The company is also working on a plan to launch multi-user warehouses. Here DotZot will pick up orders from sellers, stock them, do the packing and handle shipments.

d) *Use of Modern Technology:*
Ecom Express, cofounded last year by a group of former Blue Dart senior executives, is setting up a fully automated hub in Delhi where machines will sort packages for shipments. Logistics Companies have to invest in automation at various levels otherwise they will not be able to handle the volumes that are being projected by the Online Retailors.

The company is in talks with a Bangalore-based fashion portal to provide a service where the delivery person will wait for a customer to try out a garment, take measurements, go to a pre-approved tailor to get alterations done and deliver the altered garment to the customer. The firm, which has an employee base of over 1,300, plans to expand to over 50 more locations in the next quarter. Thus Logistic firms are trying their best to offer tailor-made services as demanded by online sites.

There are great opportunities opened to the logistic firms in this growing Online Retail Industry. The challenge for logistics firms will be to stay in step with online firms to get the maximum benefit from this emerging growth.

11.3   E-commerce is really making our lives more comfortable.

Imagine, just spending a few minutes on your smartphones, tablets, laptops, desktops, you can get anything, you name a thing under the sun, that you want at your door step within hours / days. Remember, you can get 'Services' also online.

Increased mobile penetration and smartphone adoption and internet penetration, have certainly made online shopping very easy. And Mobile Apps have made online shopping further more easily. Remember, *with our fast changing Life Style, online shopping is the ultimate solution.* So why to wait? Start online shopping now!!!

11.4   Latest Trends on Online Consumer and E-Commerce

Worldwide business-to-consumer e-commerce spending has increased tremendously in the recent years. In fact, online shopping has seen such explosive growth over the last few years that e-commerce is now outpacing brick-and-mortar businesses.

Consumer trends are evolving with the ever-growing online landscape, and without visibility into their market, online vendors will lose out on potential revenue.

Here are some 'key features' to better understand the online consumer and the growing e-commerce marketplace.

a) *Consumers can't resist a Limited-Time Sale*: According to some survey, a large number of consumers would either leave a meeting, or shop online during a meeting, to get a limited-time offer. The deals that limited-time sales some websites offer are often so attractive that consumers cannot resist them, even while in a work meeting. Oftentimes, such deals will hit a consumer's inbox in the morning hours, and by the time they get into work to check their email, an item might already be sold out. As such, limited-time sales are a foolproof way to drive website traffic.

b) *Online Shopping is a Modern Day Pastime*: More than 40 percent (223) of respondents claim to shop online on a daily basis, and nearly 30 percent (144) claim to shop online on a weekly basis. Holiday season will surely drive more consumer traffic and if unprepared, an unexpected spike in sales or even web traffic may very well lead to website slowdown or failure for their business.

'c) *Cyber Monday' lures most Consumers*: In 2013, Cyber Monday sales surpassed the sales of Black Friday, and the same trend followed suit in 2014. Consumers are continuously shifting to online shops and, as such, retailers are increasing their digital presence, especially around the holidays. Many consumers claimed to shop on Cyber Monday. In fact, Cyber Monday captures the attention of almost 90 percent of the online shoppers.

d) *Consumers 'Shop at 24 Hours of the Day'*: While many consumers shop online in the morning, the balance are split relatively even between shopping in the afternoon and in the evening. As such, e-commerce vendors need to offer their customers an always-on shopping experience, meaning their website needs to be equipped to handle traffic at any given time of day.

e) *Consumers 'welcome the Emails'*: Some e-commerce sites provide exclusive discounts for high-end brands to their members over short periods of time — generally 36 or 48 hours — drawing large numbers for each of these companies. Consumers are even willing to receive inbound emails from such e-commerce websites, to reap the benefits of the special/ super deals they offer. They also subscribe to such websites.

f) Shopping Craze rise between midnight and 6am

Some people are so addicted to shopping that many are glued to their smartphones and tablets when most of their neighbours are asleep — buying products they like, taking advantage of great deals and discount offers.

The most revealing finding of a recent study is perhaps the 30% increase in online shopping between the hours of midnight and 6am. When people know there is a bargaining, they don't care what time of day it is.

The main cause for this change is the rise of the 'tablets'. They are much more portable and comfortable that you are able to take them to bed in a way you would never have dreamed of doing with a laptop.

Shopping trends are changing very often. Now a days, set-top boxes, camcorders and iPod docks have become slower sellers, while fitness gadgets are flying off the virtual shelves. And believe it or not, sales of wearable tech devices such as the Fitbit are up nearly 900%.

The Online retail business has almost become 'a buyer's market and therefore, to become the front runner with a wide customer base and reap max profit, Online retailers have to well prepared and well equipped to meet the growing online customer expectations.

12.
CROSS BORDER E-COMMERCE

12.1   Challenges

Cross – Border E-Commerce represents a driving force, of the global marketplace, with cross-border shoppers spending approximately twice as much as consumers who only shop domestically. The finding is based on a research study on the online and cross-border shopping habits of many consumers from a large no of countries.

Various agencies have to work in tandem to smooth the path of cross-border ecommerce. The problem arises from the fact that each of these parties has a different level of understanding, motivation, and sense of urgency.

However, it is possible to overcome the challenges once you understand them. Most hurdles can be divided into the following major categories –

12.2   Regulatory Issues

a) *Inconsistency*: Business requires the bare minimum consistency in regulation. But the challenges that ecommerce is throwing at regulators is causing them to repeatedly change their mind. Even in developed countries, such as the U.S., there is debate about the applicability of state taxes on ecommerce transactions, so you can imagine the inconsistency of legal and tax regulations in less developed countries.

b) *Domestic Incorporation*: Many countries treat their domestic companies quite differently from those incorporated abroad. So if you are serious about selling to customers in a specific country, you may have to incorporate locally to take advantage of this situation.

c) **Legal restrictions to sale**: Every country has its unique set of dos and don'ts about what products can be sold to whom. Most countries consider transactions entered into by minors as unenforceable, but the exact age of legal adulthood varies by country. Similarly, several categories of products like – food, alcohol, weapons, and antiques, among others – have specific requirements. If you are shipping goods from a country that does not meet their regulations, you could be in violation of local laws in the customer's country.

d) **Lack of proper legal frameworks**: Several countries around the world have a rather weak legal framework. Even where the framework is sound, there is often a huge issue with delays in the judicial process. So, while an ecommerce player selling to another country will be bound to live up to the regulations of that country.

e) **Payment Methods and Processing**: A robust payment processing system is absolutely necessary for ecommerce. Preferred payment mechanisms vary across the world, so you need to research your potential market before you make assumptions about your payment system. You will need to accept payment in the method that the customer prefers. Other than credit cards, there is no other truly global payment method

f) **Logistics and Reverse Logistics**

Except for selling digital downloads, you have to develop a strong logistics process. Effective logistics has repeatedly proven to be a strong competitive advantage for online, as well as offline, retailers. The costs associated with cross-border logistics can be the tipping point for your ecommerce business.

It is not just about the costs. It is about reliability and predictability. You may have a logistic provider but customers believe that you are responsible for ensuring that the product reaches them. And if your delivery logistics are complex you can imagine the complexity of reverse logistics. Given the costs, customs duties, and documentation, many ecommerce players may not be able to provide reverse logistics in cross-border situations.

12.3   Cross – Border Shopping and Logistical Challenges

One of the latest and most important trends is the cross-border trading phenomenon, where consumers in one country purchase goods from nations or territories across the globe. This is a stark contrast to a decade ago when many retailers would not take credit cards with foreign addresses because payment systems did not allow for satisfactory fraud and credit card protection, not to mention the customs, duties and delivery issues that come with fulfilling foreign orders.

But as the consumer has become more global, payment solutions and retailers have aligned their efforts that appeal to all.

12.4   Other Critical issues:

a) Organizational Readiness

The business's own readiness for selling abroad is equally important. Right from an appreciation of local tastes to sensitivity for cultural factors, you must develop a deep understanding of every market you intend to tap

From the smallest ecommerce merchant to the largest big box chains, retailers of all sizes and from all countries are starting to recognize the significant global ecommerce opportunity.

Despite the list of challenges mentioned above, cross-border ecommerce presents huge business potential in growing economies around the world. A judicious approach will certainly help you to enjoy the benefits of cross-border ecommerce.

b) *Who are the Cross-Border Shoppers?*

There are people who shop domestically, cross-border and domestically, and cross-border only. But in some countries, the amount of shopping that's done cross-border is really quite significant. Cross-border shopping is really going to start to grow as an emerging market, it is said.

China has a thriving domestic market, whereas Cross-border shopping is not very prevalent in China and in many other countries right now. That is just simply because of the policies in those countries. However, China may soon become a bigger market for international trade. A large number of Chinese online consumers said they plan to begin shopping cross-border or increase their cross-border shopping in the next 12 months.

But when you look at some of the opportunities that are now opening with foreign merchants being able to sell in some of those markets that are going to really change the dynamic.

c) *What attracts Cross - Border Shopping?*

Multiple product availability is the factor the United States is the preferred shopping destination, according to some reports. Other factors include, looking for a better value, or looking for unique products. The U.S. and China are really leading the charge in terms of shopping destinations for people across the globe. What people are buying once they do decide to look at a foreign website is really clothing, footwear and accessories that are the most popular followed by consumer electronics.

d) *Free Shipping is the Key to Cross-Border Shopping*

Shipping cost is of paramount importance to cross-border shoppers. More than half of those who have shopped cross-borders in the past 12 months say that delivery costs prevent them from making purchases from another country more often.

Advancements in technology are helping to open up commerce opportunities for everyone - across borders, anywhere, anytime and via any device, what we call this - The People Economy. And PayPal is leading this movement by making it easier, more secure and more intuitive for people to pay — wherever and whenever they want.

When cross-border shoppers choose how they want to pay, the top three factors are the safest way to pay, purchase protection and a more convenient way to pay. And things like loyalty points are actually quite low on the list.

e) *Emerging Markets*

According to some recent report, Cross - Border shopping trade represents a driving force, of the global marketplace, with cross-border shoppers spending approximately twice as much as consumers who only shop domestically. The finding is based on a research study on the online and cross-border shopping habits of more than 17,500 consumers in 22 countries.

U.S. and Chinese goods are the most popular overall, representing 26 and 18 percent of all online cross-border purchases, according to the study. Shoppers from North America, Latin America and the Middle East prefer American goods, while Western European cross-border shopping is dominated by German merchandise; central and eastern European consumers most often purchase from China.

United States has the minimum cross-border shoppers, largely because U.S. consumers buy from U.S. retailers, who often offer free shipping and returns and meet consumers' product availability desire.

12 .5   Cross — Border E-commerce: Shopper's Concerns

a) *A major area of concern is reputation.* Cross-border shoppers seek out specific products rather than particular online merchants, but they want to do business with companies that they trust will provide smooth transactions and delivery of authentic goods.

b) *Consumers seek good deals around the globe.* Their biggest concerns and poorest experiences involve logistics, such as receiving the item ordered in a timely and cost- effective manner.

c) *Cross-border shoppers prefer multi-brand retailers and online marketplaces.* As a result of their concerns, cross-border shoppers prefer to purchase from well- known major multi-brand retailers and global online marketplaces.

d) *Shipping-related concerns are paramount when considering cross-border purchases.* Consumers have a variety of concerns with cross-border purchases, regardless of whether or not they've actually experienced them firsthand, ranging from shipping cost to transaction fraud.

e) *Many cross-border shipping issues are based on experience.* Long delivery time and high shipping cost are the two main problems that shoppers have experienced when making cross-border purchases

f) *Duties and taxes curb cross-border activity.* While shipping cost and delivery time are top of mind with shoppers, duties and taxes are also a factor.

Besides the above issues, other areas of concerns and problems include –

   * Fake and or inferior products,
   * Inability to return an item without added cost or hassles,
   * Damaged products,
   * Transportation security threat,
   * Shipping reliability
   * High cost of Duties / Taxes,
   * Customs delays and
   * Securities issues with my personal and payment
information.
While global shoppers may generally behave in similar ways, there are also clear differences among and within regions. However, realizing cross –border e-commerce is the latest online shopping trend affecting the world economy, countries should take initiative to resolve these issues.

13.
INTERNATIONAL PARCEL FORWARDING SERVICE

13 .1   A Solution to Cross Border Online Shoppers?

Want to shop from Amazon, Ebay, Walmart, BestBuy.... and get the parcels delivered right to your doorstep no matter where you live?

International Parcel forwarding Service is a new service emerged, offered by shipping companies to international online shoppers who want to do cross-border online shopping. Package forwarding is becoming more and more popular among international shoppers nowadays because of the high growth rate of e-commerce websites and shipping limitations of most such websites in many countries.

There are several obstacles towards a successful cross-border online shopping, which include paying for orders and shipping. For instance, US online stores are popular worldwide, but some of them only ship to US addresses or they ask for high shipping international rate.

Parcel forwarding service is provided by package forwarders to make cross-border shopping convenient and easy, getting rid of the problems of payment and shipping. A parcel forwarding service is different from mail forwarding. Mail forwarding refers to the mails in traditional meaning, or magazines or papers that are normally called mails, while parcel forwarding refers to the online purchases or orders that are shipped within a package.

There are parcel forwarding service providers from different countries and asking for different prices for their services. Choosing a reliable package forwarding service is of great importance for a happy international shopping experience.

13 .2   What Services do they provide?

Cross – Border E-Commerce has become a driving force of the global marketplace with cross-border shoppers spending approximately twice as much as consumers who only shop domestically.

Parcel Forwarding Services offer their services to international online shoppers who want to do cross-border online shopping, making it easy and hassle free. And this Service is becoming more and more popular among international shoppers nowadays because of the high growth rate of e-commerce websites and shipping limitations of most such websites.

13 .3   How do they work? These services simply give you a US address or in some cases UK, EU, Australia and Japan address options when you sign up with them. Once you sign up with them, you can use that shipping address at Amazon, Ebay, BestBuy, stores etc. to ship your purchases to your new address. Depending on the level of service they provide, the Parcel Forwarding Service will ship the item you purchased to your home country at your designated address.

An international Parcel Forwarding Service works normally with the following five steps:

     a) After you create your account with an International Parcel Forwarding Service, you will receive your new address, as per your request.
     b) The customer places an online order and asks the seller to ship the purchases to the Parcel Forwarding Service's warehouse.
     c). Parcel Forwarding Service receives your item, handle the packages, such as repacking, consolidation or storage and also

informs the shopper.

     d). Shoppers now pay the Parcel Forwarding Service for package handling and international shipping fee.

     e) The Parcel Forwarding Service ships out the item and online shoppers receive the parcel at their home..

Many parcel-forwarding companies offer additional services like repacking, inspecting, and photographing the contents, and consolidating multiple parcels into one shipment. This can save shipping costs, especially using couriers that charge more on size than weight.

14

SCARED OF ONLINE SHOPPING – WHY?

Yes, there are many people who have concerns about shopping on the internet, even with the biggest website. And if you have not done any online shopping till now, there must be some reason. Let's get the *Fear* out of their mind.

Conventional Shopping v/s Online Shopping? Generally, if you want to buy something, you visit a retail shop, buy whatever you want, pay the cash and carry the items with you. Whereas, 'Online shopping' is a process in which a customer places his/ her requirements of shopping and order them online with the help of internet facility to an Online retail store and make the payment according to their payment options. The online retail store will then deliver those items you have ordered to your address.

Technology has changed our life style and people are leading a faster and busier lives, and are finding less time for everything, especially for shopping. And with our fast changing Life Style, online shopping is the ultimate solution. It offers fast, easy, time saving, money saving and gives you very interesting and exciting shopping experience. The best advantage of online shopping is that it gives you 24 hours shopping facility. And you can do your complete shopping from your home, anywhere and anytime and then you will also have a large variety of quality products to choose from.

Furthermore, online shopping is a medium/ lifeline for all those aged, living by themselves to get their requirements to their home and for those who are away from their family and friends, to send gifts and other items to their family and friends. Isn't it just amazing?

Your concerns: You may be worrying about,

       * Fear of Credit card Information being stolen, and will my money be drained off by someone?
       * Will have to share some of my personal information, which may be misused,
       * It may not be a real store on the ground,
       * Will the products be similar to what is exhibited on their site?
       * Not able to track your orders,
       * Can the products be returned if found defective or unsuitable?
       * There must be a help line no. where you can clear your doubts about, Product information, shipping information, assistance in placing an order, expected time of delivery, etc.
       * What do I do if the online site not delivering the goods ordered even after making the payment?

15.
TIPS AND TRICKS

Just follow these Tips n Tricks for a safe online shopping.

* Try to identify a *Trustworthy* site for your online shopping. Check their identity, location, contact details, check their billing, guarantees, goods return policy, and also delivery system. This information you can get yourself or by asking your friends, checking the site's global ranking. If you are unfamiliar with the site, then you may test the site with an inexpensive purchase to begin with.

* Ensure you have an internet connection to your mobile, Laptop and Desktop etc., or you can use the internet café facilities.

* Identify the products you want to buy and be sure what you want to buy.

* Check for the discounts and special offers of the site. Here you can take the help of good 'Price Comparison sites'.

* Always use a Secured Payment System. Now a days, you get many payment options like COD (Cash on Delivery), Net banking, Credit Card Payment etc. Preferably use a Credit Card with Online Fraud Protection. For a safe operation it is advisable to keep a separate account with a reasonable balance for all your online shopping operations so that even if someone hack your account details, you will only loose whatever minimum amount lying in your that particular account.

* Always agree on the total amount that is going to be on your credit card and never allow open-ended credit charges.

* If ETA is intimated to you then be sure you are physically present at the given delivery address.

* In case the goods ordered are not delivered within the delivery schedule you should inform the police and initiate a complaint.

* Begin your cross border online shopping only after you become well versant with the online shopping system.

* Also be careful while entering your personal information,
* It is always wise to read the company's Privacy Policy.
* And don't forget: always keep a record of your purchase details.

16.
KNOW YOUR CONSUMER RIGHTS

Global e-commerce sales are growing and to no one's surprise, fraud is growing too. Online shopping has both plus and minus points. Plus points include – time saving, money saving, product choice, shopping convenience, etc. And the minus points include - frauds and cyber-crimes committed against e-commerce users. At times there are disagreements and dissatisfactions among buyers that cannot be resolved using traditional litigation methods.

Therefore, many countries in the world are now making / refining their cyber laws so that people of their country are protected against e-commerce frauds especially while doing online shopping.

Trade commissions of almost all countries have laws to protect their countrymen from being cheated either by their own countrymen or from other countries. It includes information about, Consumer Information, Consumer Rights, Consumer Protection Laws, and about, how to file a complaint etc.

In your own interest, you must learn about them, which would become very handy in case you face any problem with regard to your online shopping.

You can also get access to their videos, which are self-explanatory.

So, now you know what to do if something goes wrong with your online shopping. Make your online shopping is always hassle free and a thrilling experience.

17.
OTHER POINTS IN GENRAL

17 .1   Advice to the Online Shoppers

Always don't go after deals/ offers and other attractive discounts offered by the online retailers and low priced products, you may be cheated. More so, everyone is doing business to make some profit and not to run into loss. So if you find the online offer is much lower and unbelievable then don't buy it from that online retailer, chances are that you will be getting some fake/ grey market products. And never be price conscious all the time, but ensure you get quality products at a reasonable price. Further, you must immediately report such incidence to the appropriate authorities in your country for action against culprits.

17 .2   Buy Things which You Really Need

Many online retailers have special offers commonly known as 'Compo Offers', where a few related items are grouped and showcased with attractive discounts. For example, you are going to buy a swimming suit but order a swimming suit, a pair of swimming glasses and a cap at a 'Compo offer' price. Actually, you may already have a pair of glasses and a cap, and now you have two of each, which are really not needed.

So the point to remember is whenever you come across some 'compo offers', you must analyze the offer and buy only if all the items covered under the offer are really useful to you. Or else it will be a waste of money.

17 .3   Never get addicted to online shopping

After reading through the information about online shopping on my blogs, I am sure some of you must have decided to feel the online experience and tried to do some online shopping. And certainly most of you had a safe online shopping where as some of you would have had some bad experience and would have tried out again and became quite successful in online shopping. Now you want to have more online shopping experience.

This is a tricky situation. Because, you want to do online shopping for many reasons —

* May be you have a genuine requirement, or
* May be, you are quite excited about online shopping, or
* May be, you are attracted by the big deals / special offers the online retailers place before you, or
* May be, you are crazy to create some record for doing maximum number of online shopping etc.

Another thing is that where you could have purchased a few items together online, you try to split them and try to do online shopping either from the same site or from different sites without realizing that it is going to cost you much more than had you purchased all your requirements together and you also could have received some additional benefits on the total value of your purchases you made.

So, the bottom line is, you should do online shopping only for your genuine requirements and not get some fancy feelings. Before online shopping, you must be very sure of what you want to buy and your budget and never get attracted by the deals and special offers the online retailers announce from time to time to attract more customers to their sites.

Remember, it's you money. Don't spend it just like that, save it. It will help you in your hard time. So, *never get addicted o online shopping.*

17 .4   Motivators and Barriers for Online Shopping

What attract the consumers to do online shopping are the motivating factors. And the TOP FIVE motivating factors are:

* Fast delivery
* Ability to pay Cash on Delivery,
* Substantial Discounts as compared to the market,
* Access to Branded Products,
* Cash Back Guarantee on quality/ on faulty bills.

On a similar note, there are some important factors that prevent the consumers from doing online shopping. What are those factors? The TOP FIVE barriers preventing consumers from online shopping are:

* Freedom to touch and try the products before buying,
* Ability to return faulty products in the market,
* Immediate access to the products purchased,
* Unwillingness to post personal or financial details in the internet,
* Possibility to Bargain and to get a better deal.

Online retailers who understand the concern and expectations of the consumers and take appropriate action to *ensure quality products at a better price with an effective delivery system* will certainly attract more consumers to their online marketing sites.

Remember, consumer satisfaction / gaining consumer confidence is a MUST to drive further growth in the online retailing industry.

18.
WHO RULES THE ONLINE SHOPPING WORLD—
Men or Women?

It has always been a battle between the sexes everywhere. Most people cry for gender equality, but are they really equal? Now that 'Online Shopping' is the talk of the day, let's take of 'Online Shopping' only. Most men claim of having a love-hate relationship with shopping, especially when it comes to online shopping.

Here are some interesting findings based on surveys conducted by some of the agencies across the world. There are more women who do online shopping than men. This is a testament to the fact that women just love to shop. Women love a really good bargain and they don't hesitate to look for one.

Whoever said that gadgets are solely for boys and shoes are solely for girls had it all wrong? Women adore mobile applications. Social Media is a very, very helpful tool.

Now have a look at the 'Gender Behavior'

In a span of 30 days, 68 % men did online shopping as compared to 72 % women.

Men are more likely to find a product while browsing without having a clear destination in their mind, whereas women may be more likely to search for Brands.

On an average, women take about 14 mins to complete a purchase v/s just 10 mins for men.

Men are more likely to buy 'expensive items' as compared to women who buy less expensing items.

Women are more actively hunt for 'Bargains and Deals' and also use 'Coupons' for their online shopping as against their counterpart men.

The favoured online shopping category for men is computers, while women prefer books and both prefer buying CDs.

Men are more likely to purchase 'Travel related service' than women.

Studies show that some women will spend around three times as much on 'clothing' than men over the course of their life time. But now, some male shoppers appear to spend more on 'Shoes' than women.

Women appeared to have overtaken men on 'purchase of electronic items'.

And about 'Mobile devices and Aps', the findings are even more interesting. Women install much more Apps than men, buy more 'paid apps' than men.

On the Social Media — women are more likely to recommend a brand, product or service for the benefit of others.

Not only that more women than men share their online purchasing activities on the Social Media.

Well, there is nothing to get perturbed over the 'Gender War'. This is only a beginning and the Gender War will continue. These findings will keep change according to the new trends in online shopping. And we can look forward to more interesting and wonderful findings in future.

19.
E-COMERCE GAINING NEW HEIGHTS –
The Secret of Success

For consumers around the globe, the most well-known form of e-commerce falls into the Business to Consumer (B2C) category, also known as online retail or online shopping. It is a growing business around the globe today. E-commerce has been steadily growing gaining momentum globally in the recent years, and as per the forecast, it's expected to hit nearly $330 billion by 2016, up from $200 billion in 2011. Everything is happening so fast at an unbelievable speed. There are many factors that made 'Online Shopping' into a reality.

a) Accepting the need/ benefits of Online Shopping:
With our fast changing Life Style, online shopping is the ultimate solution. It is fast, easy, time saving, money saving and gives you very interesting and exciting shopping experience. The best advantage of online shopping is that it gives you 24 hours shopping facility. And you can do your complete shopping from your home, anywhere and anytime and then you will also have a large variety of quality products to choose from.

Furthermore, online shopping is a medium/ lifeline for all those aged, living by themselves to get their requirements to their home and for those who are away from their family and friends, to send gifts and other items to their family and friends. Isn't it just amazing?

b) The Mobile Revolution:
Increase in mobile subscribers can be attributed to the surge of low cost mobile phones and the cheaper tariffs brought on by the

intense competition between operators. Online retailers' growing reach in non-metro cities has become possible by the rise in usage of mobile internet. Increased mobile penetration and smartphone adoption in these areas is certainly one of the major factors driving this trend. Mobile Apps have made online shopping further more easily.

The mobile revolution – was big land mark in E-commerce growth. Commerce on smartphones is expected to skyrocket from $3 billion in 2010 to $31 billion in 2016, according to some other forecast.

c) Increased Internet Penetration:
Broadband penetration has also increased with the growth and development in both fixed and wireless broadband connections. Apart from internet penetration, the rise in smartphone usage, digital literacy, and purchasing power have seen online retail grow exponentially.

d) Web Content Search in local Languages:
The web content search in different languages has really boosted the mobile shopping. To highlight the effect, web content search in Hindi has grown a whopping 155 per cent in the past year in India, which is significantly higher than the growth of content search in English. And Hindi content searched through mobile Internet grew at even higher rate of 300 per cent in the same period. Growth in traffic in other languages, was also impressive.

e) Younger Demographics:
The youngest population in the 15-35 years age group is one of the largest consumer markets in the world. This population is wired, has access to smartphones and internet and is driven by the convenience of online shopping.

f) Realizing the value of Time:

Technology has changed our life style and people are leading a faster and busier lives, and are finding less time for everything, especially for shopping. Most of the people spend a significant amount of their time at work and at home with access to internet-enabled devices. And by shopping online, they save a lot of their time which they would have otherwise spent in travelling and at traffic blocks. This concept has really contributed heavily for the growth of E-commerce.

g) Cross Border E-commerce:

Emerging new technologies have made it possible for cross-border E-commerce. This helps people to do online shopping from other countries besides your own country, making it possible to buy products of your choice from across the world. But the challenges it faces now are to be resolved to make it more effective and beneficial to the people across the world, which will boost the growth of E-commerce further.

h) Factors leading to the Success?

Necessity is the mother of invention. And that's how the E-commerce came into being. Advent of Information Technology (IT) and other innovative technology, really helped to transform /make our life more comfortable.

j) Technology

Technology is the major contributor *for the growth of E-commerce/ Online Shopping* – Custom software for Online Retail Websites – Use of Hardware – Desktop – Tablets – Smartphones – Apps for easy accessibility – Internet connectivity.

k) Web Content Search in local Languages:

The web content search in different languages has really boosted the mobile shopping. To highlight the effect, web content search in Hindi has grown a whopping 155 per cent in the past year in India, which is significantly higher than the growth of content search in English. And Hindi content searched through mobile Internet grew at even higher rate of 300 per cent in the same period. Growth in traffic in other languages, was also impressive.

l) Younger Demographics:
The youngest population in the 15-35 years age group is one of the largest consumer markets in the world. This population is wired, has access to smartphones and internet and is driven by the convenience of online shopping.

m) Customer expectations:
Consumer expectations regarding time-saving, personalized service and comfort supported by new technologies are greater than ever. Online Shoppers' choice changed from – Conventional Online Shopping to – Showrooming – Webrooming – Click n Collect – Omni channel shopping, like:

n) Showrooming – A shopper visits a store to check out a product but then purchases the product online from home.

o) Webrooming – on the other hand, consumers research products online before going into the store for a final evaluation and purchase.

p) Click & Collect – A process by which the consumer is able to order online (click) and pick up (collect) their merchandise at a local store or collection point. It is a combination of online and in-store shopping and means the customers can search and buy their products on the internet and pick them up from a location of their

choice.

The Secret of Success:

As our life style changes, thanks to the *technology*, which has always been stretching beyond our imagination, we love *to make our life more comfortable*. And every one of us contributes towards this goal.

We all know, '*Time is the essence of everything*' and we are all looking for some '*Quality Time*'. But how do we find 'Quality Time'? In a way, *online shopping helps you to find some Quality Time* because by doing online shopping from your home at your convenience saves lot of your time and wasteful time you spend in traffic jams.

It is the **collective effort**, *where there was a Desire to do well, Contribution, big or small, from different sections of the community, Technological contribution, Customers growing expectations, support from the Social Networking Media and working hard to realize those dreams. And that's the Secret of Success.*

But we are yet to reach the Peak of Success. With technology stretching beyond our imagination, and with more and more people beginning to shop online, the growth of E-commerce has become quite unpredictable.

And now with 'Visual Commerce Market' using the latest technology, we are moving into a wonder-world of shopping. This technology "*allows you to walk-through any store and shop while sitting at home, bringing back the real-life shopping experience*'," while maintaining the best in class customer service.

20.
THE FUTURE?

The Future?

The points mentioned above are some of the major factors taking E-commerce momentum to greater heights. There may be predictions based on certain calculations, but we are yet to feel the real growth and challenges for Online Retail business. But it is also a fact that, with emerging new technologies and the way online retailers are taking on demanding challenges of their customers, E-commerce has a very bright future and will continue gaining its momentum.

With the support of creative, innovative and sophisticated technology, more and more people joining the group of online shoppers, the countries enforcing the regulatory system to protect their countrymen from fraud n fake products, e-commerce in general and online shopping in particular will continue to gain greater heights beyond our calculations and predictions.

******

Lightning Source UK Ltd.
Milton Keynes UK
UKIC031348171219
355509UK00013B/134